The One and Only Sam

A Story Explaining Idioms for Children with Asperger Syndrome and Other Communication Difficulties

AILEEN STALKER

Illustrated by Bob Spencer

Jessica Kingsley Publishers
London and Philadelphia

First published in 2010
by Jessica Kingsley Publishers
116 Pentonville Road
London N1 9JB, UK
and
400 Market Street, Suite 400
Philadelphia, PA 19106, USA

www.jkp.com

Library of Congress Cataloging in Publication Data
Stalker, Aileen.
 The one and only Sam : a story explaining idioms for children with Asperger syndrome and other communication difficulties / Aileen Stalker ; illustrated by Bob Spencer.
  p. cm.
 ISBN 978-1-84905-040-1 (alk. paper)
 1. Autistic children--Language. 2. Learning disabled children--Language. 3. English language--Idioms--Study and teaching (Elementary) I. Title.

 RJ506.A9S728 2010
 618.92'858832--dc22

                       2009024447

British Library Cataloguing in Publication Data
A CIP catalogue record for this book is available from the British Library

ISBN 978 1 84905 040 1

Printed and bound by Sun Fung Offset Binding Co., Ltd.

For Andrew, Patrick and Stephanie, and baby Nolan, and all the children with whom I worked and played during a wonderful career as an Occupational Therapist.

How to Use this Book

In any language, the use of idioms adds richness and uniqueness to verbal communication. However, idioms can also create problems in understanding since their real meaning is different to their literal meaning. Children usually learn to interpret idioms through the use of contextual clues and from adult explanations. However, for some children, in particular for children with communication or social learning difficulties or for whom English is a second language, misinterpretation of the words may continue. Idioms that also contain a feeling aspect create added difficulty for children who struggle to understand the meaning and intent of emotions.

This book provides a story and pictures which show both what the idioms "sound like" and then what they "really mean." It then gives a written explanation with any feeling aspect of the meaning written clearly in capital letters. Covering up the picture of the real meaning of the idiom while the child and adult look at the picture of what it sounds like and discuss its possible meanings will help with retention and understanding. The list of idioms following the story presents a chance for children to draw their own pictures to represent each of the literal and intended meanings, and to discuss any feeling aspects related to the idiom. The text also provides opportunities for children to develop perspective-taking skills and talk about the feelings and social interactions of other children.

Use of the strategy suggested by Sam and his parents to explore further idioms will help children develop the ability to visualize the sayings and to look for a match between the mental pictures they create and the explanation of the idiom.

THE ONE AND ONLY SAM

When little Sam was born, he thought the world was a wonderful place. As his Mother walked him round the streets in his baby carriage he could hear the birds sing and see the flowers blooming. Every day people stopped and said to his Mother, "What a beautiful baby!" Sam smiled and said, "Goo goo," and his Mother replied, "I love you, my one and only Sam."

But as Sam got older and began to understand more
of what people were saying, he noticed something very unusual.
When people spoke they said some very silly things.

One rainy morning after breakfast, his Mother said to his Father,
"My goodness, George, *it is raining cats and dogs* outside."

"That's strange," thought Sam. When he looked up
into the sky outside, he couldn't see any cats and dogs
anywhere, no matter where he looked. All he could see
were giant raindrops and big puddles.

Later that evening as his Mother was serving supper, she said,
"This pasta sauce is from Mrs. Roma. She would *give
the shirt off her back* if she thought we
needed it!"

   "But wouldn't she get cold?"
asked Sam, looking
puzzled.

"Oh no," laughed his
Mother. "What *give the shirt
off her back* really means is that
she is a very KIND and THOUGHTFUL
person who would do anything she could to help us."

"Ahhh," said Sam, still slightly confused. "Well I really
like Mrs. Roma. She makes great tomato sauce!"

Then his Father began talking about work. "I'm so happy my presentation went well. I feel *on top of the world* today."
"Why, Dad? Did you have to go to the North Pole for your work?" asked Sam.
Sam's Father laughed. "No, of course not—I was in my office," replied his Father. Once again, Sam looked confused.
Sam's Mother and Father smiled.

"With silly sayings like this, Sam," explained his Mother, "you have to make a picture in your mind about what the person is saying. Then ask how the people or animals in the picture might be feeling. Or think about what might be the same about the picture in your mind and what you know is really happening. Sayings like this, where the words say one thing but they mean something else are called IDIOMS."

"Think about the saying *on top of the world*, for example," continued Sam's Father.

"Usually people think of the North Pole as the top of the world. It was a lot of work for explorers to get to the North Pole. The explorers who did that first trip felt very pleased and proud of what they had done.

In the same way,
when I felt *on top of the
world*, I felt PLEASED and PROUD
of what I had been able to do at work."

"Now think about the saying *it is raining cats and dogs*. Can you work out what it means, Sam? Just use these simple steps."

1. Listen to the words.
    It is raining cats and dogs.

2. Make a picture in your mind about what the words sound like they are saying.
    Cats and dogs coming down from the sky and landing on the grass and on people and into puddles.

3. Think if this makes sense—would this ever happen? If not, what would it be like if this did happen?
   It would be very unusual if cats and dogs fell out of the sky. But if they did, you wouldn't be able to see anything but them, and they would feel very heavy when they fell on you!

4. Look for the things that are the same between what the words sound like and what is really happening.
   If it is raining really heavily, you can hardly see anything and the rain drops are big and heavy! So raining cats and dogs means it's raining very heavily.

"Sometimes," added Sam's Mother, "there is also a story from long ago to explain an idiom. For example, sailors used to think that cats had a big effect on the weather and seeing one might mean there would be a rainfall. The dog was a symbol for wind storms. So if it was raining cats and dogs it was a heavy rain with wind."

"Boy!" said Sam. "You really have to be *on the ball* to figure these idioms out!"

"Oh no!" he laughed. "What I meant was you have to be SMART and ALERT. Even I am saying them now! I hope I will understand all of them when I start school."

Soon that time came and Sam was old enough to go to school.
On the first day Sam was nervous and didn't want to go.
He wanted to stay at home with his Mother and run
and play in the park like he usually did.
As they were walking to school, Sam
thought that all the other children
looked like they were happy to
be going to school. But he just
wanted to *bury his head in
the sand*.

To *bury your head in the sand* means to ignore or avoid something that you do not like, something that makes you feel WORRIED or SCARED. If you buried your head in the sand you would not be able to see what was bothering you, but it would not be a safe thing to do and it would certainly not make the scary thing go away.

Then Sam met his teacher, Miss Smiley. She was pretty and smart, and on that very first day helped him learn to read some new words. Sam immediately loved Miss Smiley. He would have *bent over backwards* to do whatever she asked.

To *bend over backwards* means to be HELPFUL and
THOUGHTFUL when helping someone with a difficult task.
Bending over backwards to do something would be awkward
so would require a lot of extra effort.

Before he knew it, the school bell rang and the first day of school was over. Sam ran out to meet his Mother, who was standing with the other parents. He heard them talking about some of the children in his class.

Serena's mother said, "I'm really glad that Serena is going to school. She has been *at a loose end* at home by herself."

Sam had noticed that even at school Serena had just wandered around the classroom and not played with the other children.

To be *at a loose end* means a person doesn't know what to do or has nothing to do. They may feel LONELY and UNCERTAIN. The saying may have come from long ago when the captain of a sailing ship would get the sailors to coil all the ropes neatly if they were not busy.

"Well, Cindy is *full of beans* and wants everyone to be her friend," said her mother.

Sam remembered that in gym class Cindy had been the girl who tried to get everyone to play a game that she knew.

If someone acts like they are *full of beans*, they are feeling ENERGETIC and HAPPY. Some beans, like Mexican jumping beans, move around when they are warm and look like they are dancing a happy dance.

"Michael is just the
opposite," said his dad. "He often
seems to have his *head in the clouds*."

Sam had watched Michael continue looking at his book and not
even try to answer when Miss Smiley had asked the class a question.

If a person has their *head in the clouds*, they are feeling UNCONCERNED and NOT PAYING ATTENTION to what is going on around them, but they may be thinking about their own ideas in their mind.

"Even though I love him a lot, sometimes Matthew can be a *pain in the neck*," admitted his father. Sam knew just what Matthew's father was talking about. Matthew had poked Sam and tried to trip him. He refused to share his toys but wanted to play with everyone else's.

If a person is a *pain in the neck*, others usually feel
ANNOYED by this person. If a person's neck is hurting this
may also make them feel annoyed.

"I worry about how Jamie is going to manage," said his mother. "He is like *a square peg in a round hole.*" Sam had noticed that Jamie never seemed to know what was going on in class and often did exactly the opposite to what Miss Smiley asked. Sam tried to help him by whispering the instructions to him, but some of the other children just laughed at Jamie.

If someone is like *a square peg in a round hole* they feel and act AWKWARD and OUT OF PLACE. If you tried to fit a square peg in a round hole it would not go in.

"Isaac is *afraid of his own shadow*," said his mother. "I hope he will learn to be braver at school."

When the school bell had rung at the end of the day, Sam had noticed that Isaac was so startled that he had seemed to leap ten feet in the air.

If someone is *afraid of their own shadow*, they are easily WORRIED or SCARED. A person wouldn't normally be scared of their own shadow, but sometimes at night the shadow of a body can look weird enough to scare a person for a minute.

Sam was glad that the first day of school was over and that his Mother hadn't said anything to the other parents about him!

The weeks at school passed very quickly. Every day Sam went to school and asked lots of questions and learned more about people and feelings and the world he lived in. Altogether there were nine children in his class and each of the children was different. He thought Miss Smiley must have to be *on her toes* all the time to remember what each child needed to learn.

If someone is *on their toes* it means that they are feeling ALERT and making a big effort just like ballet dancers do when they dance on their toes.

Even though Miss Smiley was a very patient person, with all these children
 feeling and behaving in different ways, by the end of the day
 Sam noticed that Miss Smiley often looked like
 she was *ready to tear her hair out*.

If a person is *ready
to tear their hair out* it means
they feel FRUSTRATED and UPSET.
Someone who is upset might tug or tear at
their hair when they are thinking and trying to solve
their problems, but it would hurt too much for them to pull it out!

However, every morning Miss Smiley
would return *bright-eyed and bushy-tailed* to
teach the children in Sam's class for another day.

If a person is *bright-eyed and bushy-tailed*, they feel ENTHUSIASTIC and FULL OF ENERGY. A squirrel is bright-eyed and bushy-tailed and when they find nuts to hide or run up trees, they are very energetic.

One day, as the children were heading to lunch, Miss Smiley announced that she had a surprise for them that afternoon.

"Tell us! Tell us! What is it?" shouted the children as they pushed and crowded around Miss Smiley.

She just smiled and said, "*Curiosity killed the cat*—you will just have to wait."

Curiosity killed the cat means that if a person feels really INTERESTED in something, they might do something unsafe to find out about it, and end up in trouble—just like a cat climbing up a tree, that might get stuck or fall and hurt itself. However, usually being curious just means wanting to learn about the world.

That afternoon the children raced excitedly back into class. After they had settled down in their seats, Miss Smiley told the class what the surprise was. Every week an animal would be brought to the class and the children would learn about how that animal lived, what it ate, where it came from, and anything else interesting about it. If any of the children in the class had a pet, they could bring it to class as one of the animals for the lesson.

Right away, two children put up their hands and said they had pets they could bring to school.

Isaac was first and the next day he brought in his pet snake. When he picked it up to show the class some of the children nearly *jumped out of their skin.* But Isaac was very calm and held it firmly. He told the children that snakes wiggle out of their skin and grow a new one each year.

If someone *jumps out of their skin* they feel VERY FRIGHTENED and STARTLED. If they get an extra big shock they may jump extra high, almost leaving behind their skin!

Snakes moult (shed their skin) every year but it is not because they are frightened—it replaces old scales and allows the snake to grow.

The next day
Michael brought in
his pet turtle. For the
first time ever, he didn't seem
at all shy and talked clearly and excitedly
about his pet. Miss Smiley said how nice it was to see Michael
come out of his shell. Michael told the class that a turtle goes into its shell to
stay safe if an enemy comes along and that some land turtles can live to be one
hundred years old.

If a person *comes out of their shell* they stop feeling SHY or UNINTERESTED and start talking and joining in with activities.

When a turtle is afraid it pulls its head and legs into its shell, but if it feels safe it will stick its head out from inside the shell to look around.

LAND TURTLE = TORTOISE

When Sam went home that day he looked sad and worried.

"What's wrong, my one and only Sam?" said his mother, looking concerned. "Are those idioms upsetting you again?"

"No, no," said Sam, "I just don't know what I'm going to take in to show and tell."

"Well, Sam, we have something special to tell you that may cheer you up. Your Father and I are *on cloud nine*. We are so happy because, guess what? You are soon going to have a baby brother or sister."

To be *on cloud nine* means a person feels VERY HAPPY or ECSTATIC. If a person could float up to the clouds that would be very special and they probably would feel happy. The number nine is thought to be a special number for many religions. Also, some interesting math can be done by multiplying by nine. Try 9 x 2. It equals 18 and the 1 + 8 from the answer equals 9! Look at the nine times table and see if this continues to happen.

"A brother? A sister? But what about me?" asked Sam. "How will you have time to play with me and listen to me and help me and talk to me?"

"Don't *go to pieces* about this," said Sam's Father.
"We will have plenty of time for you and the new baby. And you will always be our *one and only* Sam!"

When something *goes to pieces* it is very difficult to put it back together again...remember Humpty Dumpty? If a person *goes to pieces*, they feel UPSET and WORRIED and even A BIT ANGRY. This may make it difficult to talk and think about all of the parts of the problem and to find a solution.

Sam sat and thought about this for quite a while.
He stared at his Mother for a long time. Then a smile came
over his face and he walked over to her.

"Mom?" he asked. "You know for the school project?
Do you think I could take…"

More Idioms

Here are some other idioms that describe how a person may be feeling or acting. If you want to, you could draw a picture of what they sound like and then what they really mean, just as was done for the idioms in this book.

At sea—When a person sails in the middle of the ocean there is only water to look at and so they might get mixed up about where they are and which direction to sail in. If a person is *at sea*, they don't know what to do and may feel CONFUSED.

Back to square one—When a person plays games such as Snakes and Ladders, often they have to go back to the beginning (square one) if their token lands on a snake. If a person goes *back to square one*, they have to start a game or project over again and may feel VERY DISCOURAGED because they have made no progress.

Bang one's head against the wall—Ouch! It would really hurt if a person banged their head against a wall and also it wouldn't solve anything. If someone *bangs their head against a wall*, they are doing something that is not getting the results they would like and they feel FRUSTRATED.

Beside him/herself—If a person could stand beside themselves they would have two of every-thing—including troubles! If someone is *beside him or herself*, the person is feeling very UPSET and WORRIED about something in their life.

Bite the bullet—In the olden days before doctors had anesthetic for operations, the injured person was given a bullet or something hard to bite when the doctor did the operation. If a person has to *bite the bullet*, they have to deal with something that is unpleasant. They may feel WORRIED but know they have to do what is expected of them.

Blow up at someone—When the pressure inside a volcano builds up, it explodes, the top of it flies off and lava flows out of it. It is a very surprising and violent event. If a person *blows up at someone*, they are feeling VERY ANGRY and may all of a sudden use angry words and actions.

The cat has your tongue—A cat usually likes to play with a toy mouse or a ball of yarn. If it was playing with your tongue, you wouldn't be able to talk. (Don't try this—cats might scratch your tongue!) If a person is asked if *the cat has their tongue* they may be feeling SHY and not talking.

Champ at the bit—A horse that has been standing too long will chew on the bit (a part of the harness) in its mouth. If a person finds themselves *champing at the bit* it means they are RESTLESS and feeling IMPATIENT.

Get carried away—When an object is thrown into a river, the current carries it away and it may get lost. Sometimes events are so exciting that people lose control of their feelings. If a person *gets carried away* they may show their feelings in many ways (crying, shouting) or do something they would not normally do. They may feel EXCITED or OUT OF CONTROL.

Get cold feet—Long ago this phrase was used to indicate that someone was poor as they could not afford to buy shoes. Later it was used about people who gambled and decided not to bet at the last minute in case they lost money. Today if a person is said to get cold feet, it means they are feeling WORRIED and SCARED about something that they are supposed to do.

Get out on the wrong side of bed—If it is a person's habit to get out on the same side of the bed each day, they may bump into things or not feel right if they get out on the other side one morning. A person who does *get out on the wrong side of bed* may feel GRUMPY and IN A BAD MOOD.

A fish out of water—If a fish flopped out of water onto the grass it would not know what to do because it couldn't swim around like it normally would. A person who feels like *a fish out of water* feels AWKWARD and ANXIOUS because they do not have the skills to manage the uncomfortable situation in which they find themselves.

Get in a stew—A stew is a dish with meat and vegetables all mixed up and it is difficult to sort out all the different bits. When a person gets worried or upset it is often difficult to sort out all the things that make the problem and think about how to solve it. If a person *gets in a stew*, it means they feel WORRIED and UPSET and CONFUSED.

Get one's wires crossed—If someone crosses the wires in an electrical appliance it probably will not work. A person who *gets their wires crossed* has misunderstood what others expect them to do and so feels CONFUSED and UNSURE about what to do next.

Get the blues—The Blues is a kind of music that is slow and sometimes sounds sad. Colours are often used to express a feeling and blue is used to show sadness. If a person *gets the blues* they may be feeling SAD.

Get mixed up—If things get mixed up—for instance toys—then it is difficult to sort them out again. If a person *gets mixed up* inside themselves, they feel CONFUSED and do not know what to do.

Go bananas—Monkeys would get very excited if they saw a lot of bananas because they like to eat them. If a person *goes bananas* they begin acting really SILLY and perhaps feel quite EXCITED.

Go off the deep end—If a person jumps into a swimming pool they usually would think about it first rather than jump without preparing themselves. If a person *goes off the deep end* it means that they suddenly and unexpectedly begin acting OUT OF CONTROL and feel ANGRY.

Go stir-crazy—To stir something means to move it around. If a person has to stay in one spot for a long time they might "go crazy" or be upset from being inactive. If someone *goes stir-crazy* they become RESTLESS and feel ANXIOUS because they have been kept in one place for too long. "Stir" is a word prisoners sometimes call the jail. Prisoners often become *stir-crazy* because they are locked in one spot for a long time.

Hit the ceiling (or roof)—If an explosion or rocket went off in a room it would hit the roof. If a person *hits the ceiling or roof*, they feel so ANGRY that they might start yelling and they might jump up and down and almost hit the ceiling.

Hot under the collar—If a person wears a tight collar on a shirt or coat they often will feel hot and irritable. To be *hot under the collar* means that person feels ANGRY or thinks something that has happened to them is UNFAIR.

Like a sitting duck—A duck that sits on the ground is an easy target for hunters. If a person is *like a sitting duck*, other people may take advantage of them. The person may feel HAPPY because they may not realize that they are at risk of being tricked or teased, or they may realize they are going to be teased or made fun of and feel WORRIED.

Lock horns with—Some animals such as moose or goats get their horns or antlers locked together when they fight. If a person *locks horn with* someone else they feel ANNOYED with someone and often they get into a long argument with that person.

At a loss for words—Sometimes when something unexpected or upsetting happens a person will try to think of what would be a useful thing to say. Because they can't find the right words—are *at a loss for words*—to say that would be helpful for the situation they may feel AWKWARD.

More fun than a barrel of monkeys—Someone who is this much fun would be a great friend. *More fun than a barrel of monkeys* means that a person feels and acts in an ENTHUSIASTIC and FUNNY way—just like a group of monkeys playing together.

My one and only—If a person has only one of something (perhaps a brand new shiny coin) it may be very special. If a person is told they are someone's *one and only*, the person feels very AFFECTIONATELY toward them.

Run wild—Wild animals can run and do whatever they want. If a person *runs wild* it means that the person is feeling so EXCITED that they are acting OUT OF CONTROL.

Quake in one's boots (or shoes)—If an earthquake happened a person might be shaking (quaking) in their shoes and it would be a scary event. If a person *quakes in their boots*, they feel AFRAID about what is happening, and are shaking.

Sore loser—When they lose a game, some people may feel very tense and angry inside their body and this makes their body feel sore. A person who is *a sore loser* thinks they should always win and may feel VERY ANGRY and feel that it is UNFAIR when they lose.

Wild about—If an animal is wild it does not have anything that keeps it from doing what it wants to do. If a person is *wild about* something they feel VERY ENTHUSIASTIC about it and talk and show others about the thing they are interested in.

Additional Resources for Understanding Idioms and their Origins

Books

Brennan-Nelson, D. (2003) *My Momma Likes to Say*. Chelsea, MI: Sleeping Bear Press.

Brennan-Nelson, D. (2004) *My Teacher Likes to Say*. Chelsea, MI: Sleeping Bear Press.

Brennan-Nelson, D. (2007) *My Grandma Likes to Say*. Chelsea, MI: Sleeping Bear Press.

Collis, H. (1987) *101 American English Idioms*. Columbus, OH: McGraw-Hill.

Flavell, L. and Flavell, R. (2005) *Dictionary of Idioms and Their Origins*. London: Kyle-Cathie.

Siefring, J. (2004) *Oxford Dictionary of Idioms*. Oxford: Oxford University Press.

Stuart-Hamilton, I. (2004) *An Asperger Dictionary of Everyday Expressions*. London: Jessica Kingsley Publishers.

Terban, M. (1987) *Mad as a Wet Hen and Other Funny Idioms*. Boston, MA: Houghton Mifflin.

Terban, M. (1990) *Punching the Clock and Funny Action Idioms*. Boston, MA: Houghton Mifflin.

Terban, M. (1996) *Scholastic Dictionary of Idioms*. New York, NY: Scholastic Inc.

Terban, M. (2007) *In a Pickle and Other Funny Idioms*. Boston, MA: Houghton Mifflin.

Welton, J. (2004) *What Did You Say? What Do You Mean? An Illustrated Guide to Understanding Metaphors*. London: Jessica Kingsley Publishers.

Websites

www.listen-up.org A website developed by a speech and language pathologist that provides modules for hearing-impaired children to learn common idioms. This program uses pictures for each idiom but does not have continuity of the people/objects/animals in both the literal and real-meaning pictures.

www.idiomconnection.com A website listing common idioms in alphabetical order with both the meaning and a sentence using the idiom. This website also lists the idioms in different categories.

www.idiomsite.com A website that provides in alphabetical order the meanings of many common idioms. At least some of the explanations are posted by readers of the site rather than being provided by the website managers.

www.usingEnglish.com A website listing idioms both alphabetically and in categories. The site is designed to help learners of English as a second language.